HEALTHY HOUSING FOR ALL

How Affordable Housing Is Leading the Way

Urban Land Institute
Center for Sustainability
and Economic Performance

centerforactivedesign.org

ABOUT THE REPORT

Urban Land Institute
The Urban Land Institute (ULI) is a global, member-driven organization comprising more than 42,000 real estate and urban development professionals dedicated to advancing the Institute's mission of providing leadership in the responsible use of land and in creating and sustaining thriving communities worldwide.

ULI's interdisciplinary membership represents all aspects of the industry, including developers, property owners, investors, architects, urban planners, public officials, real estate brokers, appraisers, attorneys, engineers, financiers, and academics. Established in 1936, the Institute has a presence in the Americas, Europe, and Asia Pacific regions, with members in 80 countries.

The extraordinary impact that ULI makes on land use decision making is based on its members sharing expertise on a variety of factors affecting the built environment, including urbanization, demographic and population changes, new economic drivers, technology advancements, and environmental concerns.

ULI Affordable and Workforce Housing Council
ULI Product Councils are groups of ULI members who meet regularly to share information and best practices. The Affordable and Workforce Housing Council's mission is to share best practices and innovative solutions from a diverse group passionate about the creation, expansion, and retention of high-quality housing that is affordable for families, seniors, and individuals.

ULI Building Healthy Places Initiative
Around the world, communities face pressing health challenges related to the built environment. Through the Building Healthy Places Initiative, launched in 2013, ULI is leveraging the power of ULI's global networks to shape projects and places in ways that improve the health of people and communities. Building Healthy Places is working to make health, social equity, and wellness mainstream considerations in real estate practice. Learn more and connect with Building Healthy Places: www.uli.org/health.

Center for Active Design
The Center for Active Design (CfAD) is the leading nonprofit organization using design to foster healthy and engaged communities. CfAD's mission is to transform design and development practice to support health, ensuring equitable access to vibrant public and private spaces that support optimal quality of life.

CfAD applies its multidisciplinary expertise to empower decision makers, providing publications, original research, certification, technical assistance, and digital tools. Rather than imposing a one-size-fits-all model, CfAD collaborates with companies and communities to identify unique local priorities and to determine measurable outcomes that can inform future investment and decision making. CfAD also serves as the exclusive operator of Fitwel, the premiere global health certification system for optimizing building design and operations. Learn more at www. centerforactivedesign.org and www.fitwel.org.

REPORT TEAM

ULI Affordable and Workforce Housing Council

Joanna Frank
President and Chief Executive Officer,
Center for Active Design

Bob Simpson
Vice President, Multifamily Affordable, Fannie Mae
Assistant Chair, Affordable and Workforce Housing Council
(Blue Flight)

Jeff Foster
Principal, GGLO Design
Vice Chair, Membership, Affordable and Workforce Housing
Council (Gold Flight)

Project Leads

Matthew Norris
Senior Manager, Content, ULI

Abbie Watts
Senior Researcher, Center for Active Design

Bryan Ross
Senior Associate, Center for Active Design

Sara Karerat
Senior Analyst, Center for Active Design

Project Staff

Rachel MacCleery
Senior Vice President, Content, ULI

Billy Grayson
Executive Director, Center for Sustainability and Economic
Performance, ULI

Aysha Cohen
Senior Associate, Content, ULI

James A. Mulligan
Senior Editor, ULI

Joanne Platt, Publications Professionals LLC
Manuscript Editor

Brandon Weil
Art Director, ULI

Anne Morgan
Lead Graphic Designer, ULI

Isabel Saffon
Strategic and Urban Designer, Saffon Urban Strategies
and Design

Katteh Tongol Wong
Creative Consultant, PurpleCircle Design (Singapore)

Jes-Sy Ong
Senior Graphic Designer, PurpleCircle Design (Singapore)

Craig Chapman
Senior Director, Publishing Operations, ULI

Global and Americas ULI Senior Executives

Ed Walter
Global Chief Executive Officer

Michael Terseck
Chief Financial Officer/Chief Administrative Officer

Cheryl Cummins
Global Governance Officer

Lisette van Doorn
Chief Executive Officer, ULI Europe

John Fitzgerald
Chief Executive Officer, ULI Asia Pacific

Adam Smolyar
Chief Marketing and Membership Officer

Steve Ridd
Executive Vice President, Global Business Operations

We know from the global evidence base that healthy, affordable housing is paramount to creating thriving communities. This knowledge is being leveraged in successful, transformative projects across the U.S., providing the real estate industry with replicable case studies demonstrating the benefits to both residents and developers.

JOANNA FRANK
President and Chief Executive Officer, Center for Active Design

Hunter's Point South | Queens, New York
Related Companies, Phipps Houses, and Monadnock Construction

CONTENTS

Support for this research was provided by
the Robert Wood Johnson Foundation. The
views expressed here do not necessarily
reflect the views of the Foundation.

"Including health considerations in development is really about the sustainability of a real estate developer's portfolio: it's essential to be marketable 15 years down the road when your property will have to compete with new properties. Properties that encourage healthy outcomes through building design, walkability, and other amenities will compete better than those that don't."

Carol Naughton
President, Purpose Built Communities

Jackson Walk | Jackson, Tennessee
Healthy Community LLC

A MESSAGE FROM THE ULI AFFORDABLE AND WORKFORCE HOUSING COUNCIL

Over the past several years, in response to growing health concerns that disproportionately affect the most underserved populations, the affordable housing industry has pioneered innovative solutions to support resident health through housing design, development, and operations.

We are seeing a rise in the number of remarkable housing projects across the country that feature these innovations—projects that intentionally and overtly promote health. These celebrated projects offer many lessons to the broader housing market, and provide a blueprint for replicating successes. As the Affordable and Workforce Housing Council, we are committed to sharing these best practices to ensure the creation, expansion, and retention of high-quality housing for all.

The benefits of prioritizing health in housing are profound, and the achievements of the affordable housing industry can help guide the expansion of these efforts. Not only do the accomplishments and lessons featured here demonstrate the social impact of healthy housing, but they also clarify the financial incentives associated with implementing these strategies.

With Americans spending more than two-thirds of their time in residences, housing has a unique power to influence health and quality of life. It is our aim that the motivations, strategies, and approaches featured throughout this publication will guide housing developers to systematically prioritize health and wellness, ultimately driving transformation of the market—both affordable and market-rate.

Joanna Frank
President and CEO,
 Center for Active Design

Bob Simpson
Vice President, Multifamily
 Affordable, Fannie Mae
Assistant Chair, Affordable
 and Workforce Housing
 Council (Blue Flight)

Jeff Foster
Principal, GGLO Design
Vice Chair, Membership,
 Affordable and Workforce
 Housing Council (Gold Flight)

THE **VALUE** OF **HEALTHY HOUSING**

Developers of affordable and mixed-income housing are among the primary innovators when it comes to supporting the health needs of residents and to offering design and programming solutions to address them—but demand for healthy housing units far outweighs supply. Because of the well-understood benefits of health-focused approaches and the strong consumer appetite for healthy places, a clear opportunity exists to replicate these strategies to meet the demand and need for healthy housing at all price points.

An all-inclusive approach to health across the housing marketplace—including market-rate, middle-market, and production-built homes—presents opportunities for developers, designers, and investors to leverage demand for health-promoting building and neighborhood components, including bicycle storage areas, community gardens, and proximity to schools, shops, green space, and centers of employment.

The evidence that individuals and families increasingly value health when making housing decisions is clear. For example, access to fresh, healthy food is a top or high priority for 73 percent of U.S. residents when choosing where to live,[1] and 81 percent of millennials and 77 percent of "active boomers" believe that alternatives to driving are important when deciding where to live and work.[2]

An examination of successful health-focused affordable and mixed-income housing development examples from across the United Sates indicates that investing in high-quality, healthy project features can pay dividends. Coupled with further investment in affordable housing, market-rate developments—with features such as community gardens, fitness classes, bike- and pedestrian-focused amenities, parks and open spaces, and culturally relevant activities that emanate from the community—can play a role in mitigating place-based community health disparities, while supporting real estate project success.

RESEARCH
APPROACH

Healthy Housing for All is a joint publication of the Urban Land Institute (ULI) Building Healthy Places Initiative, the Center for Active Design (CfAD), and the ULI Affordable and Workforce Housing Council (AWHC). It includes lessons learned from:

- In-depth interviews with leading affordable housing developers and agency personnel who have focused on health through their project investments;
- Analysis of healthy affordable housing case studies;
- A review of existing evidence-based research related to the impetus, demand, and marketability of healthy housing;
- Input from roughly 100 ULI members who attended a "Healthy Housing for All" workshop at ULI's 2018 Spring Meeting in Detroit; and
- Ongoing collaboration among AWHC member leaders on this topic.

Profiles of a subset of projects identified through the research process are included in this report.

RACHEL MACCLEERY

"Healthy Housing for All" workshop | ULI 2018 Spring Meeting

HEALTHY HOUSING PROGRAMS

AND FEATURES

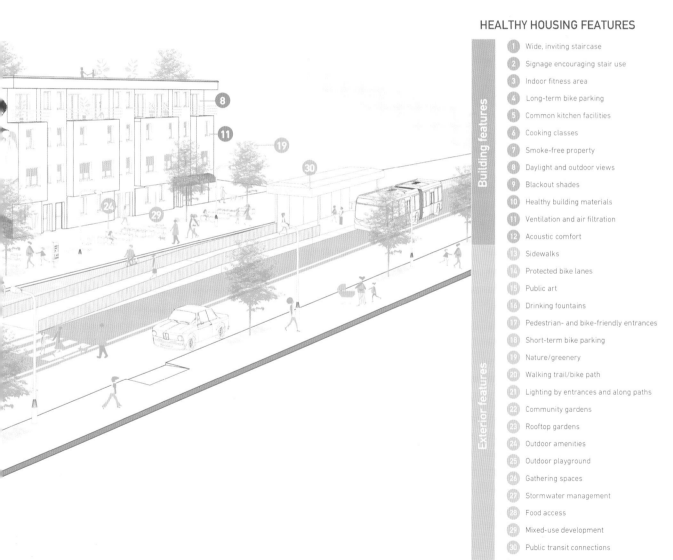

HEALTHY HOUSING FEATURES

Building features

1. Wide, inviting staircase
2. Signage encouraging stair use
3. Indoor fitness area
4. Long-term bike parking
5. Common kitchen facilities
6. Cooking classes
7. Smoke-free property
8. Daylight and outdoor views
9. Blackout shades
10. Healthy building materials
11. Ventilation and air filtration
12. Acoustic comfort

Exterior features

13. Sidewalks
14. Protected bike lanes
15. Public art
16. Drinking fountains
17. Pedestrian- and bike-friendly entrances
18. Short-term bike parking
19. Nature/greenery
20. Walking trail/bike path
21. Lighting by entrances and along paths
22. Community gardens
23. Rooftop gardens
24. Outdoor amenities
25. Outdoor playground
26. Gathering spaces
27. Stormwater management
28. Food access
29. Mixed-use development
30. Public transit connections

13. Sidewalks: Fifty-six percent of millennials and 46 percent of baby boomers prefer walkable communities.[17]

14. Protected bike lanes: A study by the Salt Lake City Department of Transportation found that replacing parking with protected bike lanes increased retail sales.[18]

15. Public art: Ninety-seven percent of real estate industry leaders agree that the developers have an important role to play in enhancing arts and culture—which can increase social connections, reflect a community's culture, and increase project value.[19]

16. Drinking fountains: Water fountains benefit the health and safety of residents as they enjoy outdoor on-site amenities.[20]

17. Pedestrian- and bike-friendly entrances: Providing sidewalks can increase transportation options for those who cannot drive or choose not to do so—such as older adults and those with physical or sensory limitations.[21]

18. Short-term bike parking: Investing in bicycling infrastructure is cost-effective and meaningfully contributes to savings on health care.[22]

19. Nature/greenery: Many studies cite the calming effects of nature and find that health can be harmed by a lack of exposure to nature.[23]

20. Walking trail/bike path: Seventy-one percent of homeowners consider proximity to trails when choosing where to live.[24]

21. Lighting by entrances and along paths: Lighting can reduce crime, ultimately benefiting neighborhood economic vitality.[25]

22. Community gardens: As of 2013, 35 percent of all U.S. households were growing food at home or in community gardens.[26] Community gardening can aid in promoting intergenerational social ties.[27]

23. Rooftop gardens: Food growing spaces can be installed on the roofs of buildings, in parking lots, or in other open spaces.[28]

24. Outdoor amenities: Outdoor amenities, such as benches and tables, are a popular and valuable residential amenity.[29]

25. Outdoor playground: Playgrounds coupled with adult-oriented fitness equipment provide opportunities for physical activity across generations.[30]

26. Gathering spaces: Seventy-four percent of landscape architects surveyed in 2018 indicate high consumer demand for multifamily outdoor amenities.[31]

27. Stormwater management: Green infrastructure can decrease energy and water costs, reduce maintenance costs, and improve occupant health.[32]

28. Food access: Up to 30 million Americans live in places with limited access to healthy food.[33] Seventy-three percent of U.S. residents indicate that access to fresh, healthy food is a top or high priority.[34]

29. Mixed-use development: Compact, mixed-use communities tend to have lower per-capita crime rates.[35]

30. Public transit connections: Fifty-two percent of Americans indicate they would like to live in a place where they seldom need to use a car.[36]

1. Wide, inviting staircase: When staircases are prominent and inviting, those without physical mobility limitations are more likely to take the stairs rather than elevators. Residents reap the health benefits of stair climbing—and building owners realize the energy savings.[3]

2. Signage encouraging stair use: Signage that encourages stair use is a low-cost strategy found to be effective in increasing physical activity for those without limited physical mobility or sensory limitations.[4]

3. Indoor fitness area: On-site gyms and other fitness- and wellness-related amenities are in high demand, with fitness centers being second only to a development's pet-friendliness in influencing project revenue.[5]

4. Long-term bike parking: Secure bike parking requires relatively little space and a limited capital expenditure, with a 14-by-6-foot space accommodating 12 bicycles.[6]

5. Common kitchen facilities: Common areas for socializing are in high demand, in particular, shared kitchens that can be used for community gatherings.[7]

6. Cooking classes: Common kitchens provide opportunities for cooking programs, which can promote healthy eating.[8]

7. Smoke-free property: Smoke-free and tobacco-free policies reduce the risk of fire and property damage and can substantially reduce maintenance and turnover costs.[9]

8. Daylight and outdoor views: Daylighting—the illumination of buildings by natural light—supports resident psychological well-being and can reduce total building energy costs by as much as one-third.[10]

9. Blackout shades: Blackout shades reduce exposure to artificial light at night, which has been linked to several negative health effects and sleep disorders.[11]

10. Healthy building materials: Sustainable healthy materials cost little to no more than conventional materials and can improve energy efficiency.[12] Substances such as lead and asbestos have long been recognized as harmful to human health.[13]

11. Ventilation and air filtration: Modest investments to enhance ventilation and minimize mold can yield significant savings for residents in the form of health care costs and missed work and school days.[14]

12. Acoustic comfort: Residents of all generations value quiet in apartment living.[15] Ninety-one percent of renters are interested in soundproof walls, and 53 percent of those interested say they will not lease without this feature.[16]

PART 2

INSIGHTS FROM AFFORDABLE AND MIXED-INCOME DEVELOPMENT PROJECTS

Members of the affordable housing industry have pioneered the practice of building healthy places for lower-income residents. These leaders are committed to creating environments and experiences that can help counteract the health inequities that too often affect low-income communities.

No standard approach exists for creating health-promoting housing. Properties come in a range of sizes and types, exist in varying climates, and are occupied by diverse tenants. However, much can be gleaned from the successes and challenges of existing affordable and mixed-income housing projects, and developers can draw from a growing number of evidence-based strategies (see pages 6–7).

The following four practical considerations for developing healthy housing for all were distilled from our research and from affordable and mixed-income projects that are leading the way:

HEALTHY HOUSING COMPONENTS IN FEATURED PROJECTS

Project	Location	Use	Active transportation features	Healthy food access or community kitchen	Fitness equipment	Active staircases	Parks and community gathering spaces	Proximity to jobs, schools, retail, services	Community events, classes
Prospect Plaza	Brooklyn, NY	Multifamily, mixed use, affordable	X	X	X	X	X	X	
Pavilion Apartments	East Orange, NJ	Multifamily affordable senior apartments		X	X		X	X	
Greenbridge	White Center, WA	Multifamily, mixed use, mixed income	X	X			X	X	X
Mariposa	Denver, CO	Multifamily, mixed income	X	X	X	X	X	X	X
New Genesis Apartments	Los Angeles, CA	Multifamily, mixed use, mixed income	X				X	X	X
Villages of East Lake	Atlanta, GA	Multifamily, mixed use, mixed income	X	X	X		X	X	X

Casitas de Colores | Albuquerque, New Mexico
Romero Rose LLS and YES Housing Inc.

IDENTIFY AND INCORPORATE
HEALTHY HOUSING FEATURES AT THE OUTSET

———

Whether new construction, renovation, or preservation, healthy housing features can be successfully incorporated in a variety of settings and at a range of scales. Certain design enhancements and programming can easily be integrated into existing projects. However, planning ahead to ensure that decisions about healthy features are made at the outset—which will help ensure that the costs remain relatively inexpensive in the overall project context—can be beneficial.

Considerations at the planning stage of new construction and rehabilitation, such as window location and material choice, can yield significant savings. Daylighting—the illumination of buildings by natural light—supports resident psychological well-being and can reduce total building energy costs by as much as one-third.[37] Sustainable healthy materials cost little to no more than conventional materials and can improve energy efficiency and indoor environmental quality.[38]

Identifying and incorporating healthy housing features at the outset also go hand in hand with engaging residents and stakeholders.

Project Profile

Prospect Plaza

Brooklyn, New York

Prospect Plaza is a mixed-use affordable housing redevelopment project spread over five buildings and three blocks in Brooklyn's Ocean Hill–Brownsville neighborhood. The $200 million project is replacing a former New York City Housing Authority complex with a mix of nearly 400 public housing and affordable rental apartments, retail space, and community and recreational facilities designed to support resident health in a rapidly developing area.

Area stakeholders—including current and former neighborhood residents, public and agency officials, and lead developer Blue Sea Development—coalesced around a vision for a new Prospect Plaza with a mix of housing types, open space, and access to fresh food and active transportation facilities after a community planning workshop organized by the housing authority in 2010.

Plans for the new Prospect Plaza centered on improving resident health outcomes—a particularly acute need, as the Ocean Hill–Brownsville neighborhood experienced the highest death rates in New York City caused by avoidable chronic health conditions as recently as 2012, according to the city's Office of Vital Statistics.

The result is a dynamic development that includes a variety of housing types, designated open space, and access to fresh food and active transportation opportunities. This vision was realized with thoughtful consideration and planning of health-promoting features from the start.

Size
4.5 acres (1.8 ha); 394 public and affordable housing units

Type
Multifamily, mixed use, affordable

Project team
Blue Sea Development, Dattner Architects, Pennrose Properties LLC, Duvernay + Brooks, Rosenberg Housing Group, New York City Housing Authority

Health-promoting highlights
Community center (10,000 square feet, 930 sq m), on-site public park (0.75 acres, 0.3 ha), retail space (23,000 square feet, 2,100 sq m), raised garden beds, indoor and outdoor exercise and recreation areas, stairways designed to encourage use, nearby public transportation, bike parking, and planned supermarket

Prospect Plaza | Brooklyn, New York
Blue Sea Development and partners

THE CENTER FOR ACTIVE DESIGN

More than 40,000 families applied for Prospect Plaza's first 110 residential units, which opened in 2016 and were reserved for families of four earning about $51,000 per year. The strong demand illustrates the need for additional healthy, affordable housing in the region.

"Projects designed to support resident health can provide much more stable environments. This increased stability not only creates a great social return in keeping families healthy, but also can support a project's financial success. A healthy building is beneficial to a building owner's bottom line.**"**

Les Bluestone
President, Blue Sea Development Company and Blue Sea Construction Co.; Board Chair, Center for Active Design

Project Profile

Pavilion Apartments

East Orange, New Jersey

Health-promoting features are not just considerations for new developments. All projects can optimize their buildings in different ways. Sites like the Pavilion Apartments illustrate the possibilities for an existing development.

The rehabilitation of Pavilion Apartments —undertaken by Vitus Group, a firm that specializes in the revitalization and preservation of affordable housing across the United States—centered on efficiently delivering a healthier living environment for building residents.

Ensuring that health-promoting strategies were incorporated into the planning phase and accounted for in budget considerations was vital, as it was essential to predetermine which healthy design strategies could be implemented in the context of an existing building.

Through detailed planning and a focus on health from the start, the cost of added healthy design features—including on-site health services, a community kitchen, garden, fitness area, and space for outdoor recreation—accounted for only about 2 percent of the project budget.[39]

The project was funded by Citi Community Capital and will remain affordable for at least 20 more years after the 2016 rehabilitation. All units are restricted to tenants earning 60 percent of area median income or less and are designated for people over the age of 62 or those with disabilities.

Size	**Type**	**Project team**	**Health-promoting highlights**
298 units	Multifamily affordable apartments for older adults	Vitus Group	On-site health services, community room, community kitchen, garden, fitness area, space for outdoor recreation

Pavilion Apartments | East Orange, New Jersey
Vitus Group

Pavilion Apartments | East Orange, New Jersey
Vitus Group

ROLAND LIM PHOTOGRAPHY

ROLAND LIM PHOTOGRAPHY

 Healthy features are cost-effective, yet developers may not always know how to move forward with including them in their projects. Ensuring that health-promoting strategies are incorporated into a project's planning phase is vital. "

Stephen Whyte
Founder and Managing Director,
Vitus Group

Silver Moon Lodge | Albuquerque, New Mexico
DBG Properties LLC

DEKKER/PERICH/SABATINI

ENGAGE RESIDENTS AND STAKEHOLDERS
AND CONDUCT RESEARCH TO ENSURE THAT PROJECTS ADDRESS THEIR PRIORITIES

———

Residents want to know how new developments are going to improve their quality of life, from food access to schools and educational opportunities. Prioritizing health from a project's start and engaging those who will be affected by a project allow the planning team to tailor the project to residents' wants and needs, which generates community buy-in. In turn, developers may be able to more efficiently receive land entitlements—zoning, use permits, landscaping, and utility and road approvals—potentially lowering the costs of development.

Affordable and mixed-income housing development teams have led the way in creating innovative processes for integrating health and community engagement. Effective strategies include (a) working with current and former neighborhood residents and other stakeholders to create comprehensive health evaluation metrics, (b) walking around an area and having casual conversations with residents rather than assuming they will show up to more formal planning and visioning meetings, and (c) translating public health research into actionable insights to increase community awareness.[40]

Other planning methods, such as a health impact assessment, can also be employed to benchmark current conditions within a neighborhood and among residents.[41] The data generated from such an assessment can be shared with the design and planning team to ensure that buildings and spaces specifically target community needs, promote good health, and mitigate negative health consequences.

Project Profile

Greenbridge

King County, Washington

Greenbridge was built to replace World War II–era public housing with a vibrant, mixed-use, and mixed-income neighborhood focused on high-quality amenities for all to use, including connections to open space, neighborhood amenities, and youth and social services.

The community is economically and ethnically diverse, with a mix of housing types at multiple price points—including rent-subsidized units, workforce units, for-sale homes, and fully accessible units with such features as lower counters and a roll-in shower.

Community engagement played a central role in GGLO Design's process. Greenbridge's design phase included simultaneous translation into six languages to ensure that the needs of local residents would be addressed in the final project.

A key lesson from GGLO Design's engagement efforts was the recognition that car ownership and use rates were well below average in this community, which provided an opportunity to rethink connectivity and dedicate more public space to biking and walking as the dominant modes. Investors were motivated to provide grants and loans for the project based in part on the thoroughness of community outreach and the quality of the resulting development plan.[42]

The extensive planning and community engagement resulted in a sustainable and active community that allows safe and convenient routes to key destinations, such as parks and neighborhood shopping areas for those who cannot drive or choose not to do so.

Size
100 acres (40 ha); 1.65 million square feet (153,000 sq m) residential; 54,000 square feet (5,000 ha) commercial; 1,100 units

Type
Mixed-income, multifamily residential community with a variety of housing choices and building types, including for-sale detached housing, clusters of single-story cottages, attached townhouses, and stacked townhouses over flats

Project team
King County Housing Authority, GGLO Design, Goldsmith, KPFF, Juan Alonso, Mary Cross, Haddad|Drugan, Steve Jensen, Seattle Solstice, Michael "Yeggy" Yegizaw, Caldweld Sculpture Studio

Health-promoting highlights
Sidewalks, trails, and paths; nearby retail centers; open spaces ranging in size; community parks; pocket parks; food gardens; recreation spaces; locally made public art to denote public gathering spaces

Greenbridge | King County, Washington
King County Housing Authority

❝The growing demand for improved amenities and healthier living environments is a source of motivation for developers. Health is an essential and recurring theme in community engagement processes.**❞**

Jeff Foster
Director of Affordable Housing,
Principal, GGLO Design

Project Profile

Mariposa

Denver, Colorado

In 2009, the Denver Housing Authority began the process of redeveloping the half-century-old South Lincoln Park Homes public housing complex—which was experiencing concentrated poverty and above-average levels of crime—into Mariposa, a new development focused on community health.

During planning, the Mariposa Healthy Living Initiative—led by the housing authority and multidisciplinary design firm Mithun Inc.—was created to comprehensively address community health throughout redevelopment. Through the initiative, community engagement efforts revealed that current residents wanted to live in a safe, walkable, mixed-use community with convenient access to healthy food and community services.

The "Mariposa Healthy Living Toolkit" was developed to help guide design and development practitioners in the planning and development of properties focused on improving health.[43]

One of the explicit goals of Mariposa was to transform a neighborhood and catalyze investment in a previously overlooked area. The project has spurred investment of a similar project in the nearby Sun Valley neighborhood in Denver, evidence that this goal has been achieved.[44] Mariposa is also now surrounded by a 24-hour grocery store, a full-service pharmacy, and eight community and conventional banks.

All units at Mariposa are finished with the same amenities, but each building houses residents with a range of income levels. As of 2018, rents range from as low as $50 to $1,700 per month.[45]

Size
17.5 acres (7.1 ha);
581 multifamily,
mixed-income units

Type
Multifamily,
mixed-income
redevelopment

Project team
Denver Housing Authority, Mithun Inc., Ross Management, U.S. Department of Housing and Urban Development, Colorado Health Foundation, Enterprise Community Partners, Koelbel and Co.

Health-promoting highlights
Neighborhood traffic calming, bike lane and access to the new on-site Denver B-cycle bike share system, tree plantings, public art celebrating the neighborhood's cultural diversity, interactive staircase, community garden, health classes and services, on-site culinary arts training for youth

Mariposa | Denver, Colorado
Denver Housing Authority

Although waiting lists for housing at Mariposa are significant, 45 percent of the residents of South Lincoln Park Homes have returned, which compares favorably with the national rate of 10 percent for similar public housing redevelopment projects.[46]

❝The community affected by our redevelopment efforts is very involved in envisioning what the neighborhood will look like. Despite excitement about new housing, a question residents had is how the new developments were going to improve their quality of life. Based on this feedback, programming such as community gardening efforts became a central design focus for the Denver Housing Authority. ❞

Ismael Guerrero
Executive Director, Denver Housing Authority

Arbor House | Bronx, New York
Blue Sea Development

COORDINATE DESIGN, POLICY, AND PROGRAMMING

C hanging the built environment and providing health-promoting policies and programs for residents are all important, and these approaches are obviously connected. To that end, embracing a multipronged approach to investing in resident health means considering the interaction between design, policy, and programming.

A multipronged approach to healthy housing development has implications for resident well-being as well as a developer's bottom line. For example, studies show that community outreach programs centered on food and health may be as important as access to a grocery store in increasing consumption of foods that support health.[47] At the same time, common areas—such as shared kitchens that can accommodate resident activities—are in high demand in multifamily projects.[48]

Developers of affordable and mixed-income housing have demonstrated successful strategies for integrating physical features, such as shared kitchens, with related programming—including cooking classes and other food-based community gatherings.

Certain policies and programs are only possible if the built structures exist to accommodate and encourage their use. Programming such as fitness, wellness, and nutrition classes and connecting to health care and social services require spaces and coordination that invite resident participation.

Project Profile

New Genesis Apartments

Los Angeles, California

New Genesis Apartments is a $36.6 million project that transformed the former Genesis Hotel, a two-story, 30-unit single-room-occupancy property built in the 1920s, into a mixed-income, mixed-use development. The building is situated in an area of Los Angeles that is home to more than 4,600 people who lack permanent stable housing.

Addressing local issues of homelessness and displacement, 75 percent of New Genesis units are allocated as supportive housing for people with a history of homelessness or chronic mental illness, and the remaining units provide affordable housing, including designated artist lofts—reflecting the focus on arts and culture in the surrounding neighborhood. Residents in supportive housing units pay no more than 30 percent of their monthly income in rent.

New Genesis offers a synchronized physical environment, services, and amenities that benefit the health and well-being of residents. For example, communal spaces are equipped to accommodate support group meetings and meditation workshops, and an on-site health clinic offers mental health and substance-abuse treatment.

Size
106 housing units; 2,400 square feet (223 sq m) of ground-floor retail

Type
Multifamily, mixed-income, mixed-use, supportive housing

Project team
Skid Row Housing Trust, Killefer Flammang Architects

Health-promoting highlights
Communal interior and exterior spaces, substance-abuse recovery center with mental health services, art workshops, natural lighting, medical clinic for primary care, bicycle parking and programming, nontoxic building materials, stormwater management features

New Genesis Apartments | Los Angeles, California
Skid Row Housing Trust

A 2016 study that tracked New Genesis residents over a four-year span showed that emergency room visits and hospitalization rates decreased significantly and that incarcerations were eliminated entirely.[49]

Anthem on 12th | Seattle, Washington
Spectrum Development Solutions

ESTABLISH INNOVATIVE PARTNERSHIPS, FINANCING STRATEGIES, AND REVENUE STREAMS

Affordable housing developers typically piece together financing from a variety of sources, including tax credits, grants, and loans. Through establishing innovative partnerships and revenue streams, many have created sustainable funding streams, such as leasing ground-floor commercial space to the community for health-promoting events, classes, training sessions, and other programming.

Capital markets and investors may also be attracted to features common in healthy affordable and mixed-income housing projects because of their social impacts. Blake Olafson, founder and managing partner at ACRE (Asia Capital Real Estate), notes, "Responsible investors aim to improve community well-being, but many social impact investments have poor returns. In contrast, including health initiatives across projects in your portfolio supports attractive investor returns due to the benefits they produce—including increasing resident retention."

Many of the approaches to partnerships, financing strategies, and revenue streams found in affordable and mixed-income housing development are relevant to market-rate development. And although the establishment of these approaches may stem from business decisions, strategic choices can be made to benefit residents living in new or renovated housing developments at all price points. Many of these choices can also serve to promote improved well-being for surrounding community members.

Project Profile

Villages of East Lake

Atlanta, Georgia

The Villages of East Lake is a project that redeveloped the former East Lake Meadows public housing complex and addressed decades of disinvestment and depopulation in Atlanta's East Lake community. A focus on education, economic development, and enhanced safety and vibrancy of the neighborhood led to significant improvements in community well-being, including a 90 percent drop in violent crime.[50]

Today, residents stay 3.5 times longer in East Lake than in similar apartments, and residents in units with deep, permanent affordable housing stay an average of seven years. Half of all units are reserved for those earning 60 percent of the area median income or below, with the rest available at market rate.[51]

A major component of the project's success can be traced to innovative partnerships and revenue streams. Project partners include the YMCA, East Lake Meadows Residents' Association, Atlanta Public Schools, Atlanta Housing Authority, and the East Lake Foundation—an organization formed to direct the East Lake Meadows redevelopment. Funding for on-site programming comes from a variety of sources, including the revitalization of a nearby golf course that hosts an annual major PGA tournament that generates 40 percent of needed revenue. The remainder is covered by public funds, fundraising, and private debt and equity managed by the East Lake Foundation.

Size

175 acres
(71 ha); 542 units;
108 additional
mixed-income
apartments planned
for completion
in 2019

Type

Multifamily, mixed
income, mixed use

Project team

East Lake Foundation,
Purpose Built
Communities (established
in 2009 to replicate the
"East Lake Model" in
other urban areas with
concentrated poverty
around the nation), YMCA,
Atlanta Public Schools,
Atlanta Housing Authority

**Health-promoting
highlights**

Community garden with job and youth training; pedestrian pathways and bus stop at entrance; sports fields, a pool, and five playgrounds; charter school; fitness classes; Early Education and Family Center; year-round career/education/recreational programming; community room with full kitchen; pedestrian lighting; grocery store

Villages of East Lake | Atlanta, Georgia
Housing Authority of the City of Atlanta and the East Lake Foundation

EAST LAKE FOUNDATION

66 It's good business to focus on the social determinants of health in housing. Partnerships that promote programs and design features that support healthy living serve to increase revenue. **99**

Carol Naughton
President, Purpose Built Communities

A central aim of the project was to retain residents and enable them to invest their time and money in the community. Residents of East Lake Meadows public housing were given priority in the new Villages of East Lake subsidized units; over a quarter chose to return.[52]

"At Fannie Mae, we know that an individual's health and well-being are closely tied to where they live, and research indicates that incorporating certain building design elements and resident services can have a measurable positive impact. These design features create healthier living environments for the individuals and families who call affordable rental properties home."

Bob Simpson
Vice President, Multifamily Affordable and Green Finance, Fannie Mae

Century Building | Pittsburgh, Pennsylvania
TREK Development Group

Incentivizing Healthy Design: Fannie Mae's Healthy Housing Rewards Program

A s all developers are aware, before a project can come to fruition, a budget must be set and financing must be secured. The outcome of these initial steps dictates limits for a project, setting the stage for what is feasible. When discussing the implementation of healthy design strategies, the first questions generally revolve around whether the budget allows for the inclusion of health-promoting features.

Healthy Housing Rewards

Based on an understanding of the opportunities for improving the health and well-being of residents at affordable rental properties, Fannie Mae launched the Healthy Housing Rewards program in 2017 in collaboration with the Center for Active Design. This program builds on the success of Fannie Mae's Green Financing programs, which issued $27.6 billion in new financing to more than 1,000 multifamily properties that met energy- or water-saving requirements in 2017 alone.[53]

Through the program's Healthy Design pathway, Fannie Mae provides a discount of 15 basis points on interest rates—and reimbursement of certification fees—for borrowers who incorporate health-promoting design and operational features into their newly constructed or rehabilitated multifamily affordable properties.[54] To qualify, borrowers must achieve Fitwel certification for their project—earning at least a 1 Star Fitwel Rating—while also meeting affordability criteria.

Market Transformation

Scalable, systemic solutions that deliberately shape financial mechanisms have the potential to elevate health, particularly for the most at-risk communities. Incentive programs like Healthy Housing Rewards have the power to shift the marketplace, influencing both supply and demand.

PART 3

Celadon at 9th & Broadway | San Diego, California
BRIDGE Housing

BRIDGE HOUSING

66 Developers unfamiliar with health-promoting features may think that these features cost more than they actually do. In reality, some features do not cost more at all, especially in the long term. Even if some features have a high upfront cost, the monthly payback is quite large for the developer and the savings are high for the residents. 99

Aruna Doddapaneni
Senior Vice President, BRIDGE Housing

THE HEALTHY HOUSING DEVELOPMENT OPPORTUNITY

The real estate industry has an important role to play in shaping the health and well-being of residents. Ultimately, healthy housing development practice contributes to long-term, sustainable real estate value, that is, healthier housing is good for both residents and business.

For developers, shifting market forces are leading to an enhanced focus on health and wellness in residential projects. Even without financial incentives like Fannie Mae's Healthy Housing Rewards program, a focus on resident health can make sense for a project's bottom line—which, in turn, increases the feasibility of additional healthy housing development at all price points.

For example, the Century Building—a mixed-use, mixed-income development in Pittsburgh, that devoted 15 percent of its construction budget to green and wellness features—was fully leased within 90 days—six months ahead of schedule. The building has also achieved a notably high 90 percent retention rate.[55]

Reasons for developers to focus on health across the housing marketplace and a variety of price points include (a) developers can capture the strong market demand for health, (b) healthy housing features are cost-effective, and (c) healthy housing supports resident stability and well-being.

DEVELOPERS CAN CAPTURE THE STRONG MARKET DEMAND FOR HEALTH

Strong market demand exists for many of the healthy features included in affordable and mixed-income housing developments, making a health-promoting approach a smart business decision.[56]

Consumers increasingly demand health-promoting amenities and programming, such as social spaces and fitness classes.[57] Eighty-five percent of Americans identify proximity to parks, playgrounds, open space, or recreation centers as central factors they look for when choosing their residential community.[58]

A focus on inclusive, healthy features—such as accessible sidewalks and multiuse trails—also presents positive implications for advancing social equity, especially given the high cost of owning, operating, and insuring a car, which averaged nearly $8,500 in the United States in 2017.[59] Residents across generations share a desire to live in places where they are not dependent on motorized vehicles to access the activities of daily living.[60]

By framing health as a priority and meeting consumer demand, developers of properties with health-promoting features can build a successful narrative that demonstrates the overall social value of a project and builds a positive reputation for the company as a whole. This message can be used to attract residents and can serve as a marketing tool to spur investment in the property and neighborhood.

Health can be marketed in many ways, and the approach selected can be tailored to the goals of the project. For example, bike-friendly developments in cities like Minneapolis with extensive active transportation infrastructure, including trails and bike lanes, respond to the local popularity of cycling.[61]

In addition, high-quality, mixed-income housing developments with health and wellness features can preserve local housing affordability, while catalyzing complementary projects within the surrounding area that include neighborhood-serving retail and services.

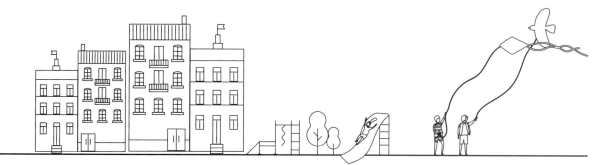

HEALTHY HOUSING
FEATURES ARE
COST-EFFECTIVE

Relatively low capital expenditures on healthy design features can support project success. Such features, and associated programs, are often also relatively inexpensive to operate once a project is built. For example, a multifamily community garden can cost as little as $5,000 to build and only $900 annually to maintain.[62] Community gardens can serve as gathering spaces, can reduce social isolation, can lead to increased resident satisfaction, and can help differentiate projects from others on the market.[63]

Developers may even be able to generate cost savings by prioritizing features to support healthier lifestyles. Silver Moon Lodge—a mixed-use affordable housing development at the periphery of Albuquerque's central business district—includes a bike-friendly design and only 23 parking spaces for 154 units, which significantly reduced the site costs associated with building parking.[64] Within a year of opening, over 95 percent of the units at Silver Moon Lodge were occupied and the building is consistently nearly fully leased.[65] This situation supports the bottom line, since unit vacancies negatively affect a project's return on investment.

Modest investments to enhance ventilation and minimize mold can yield significant savings for residents in the form of lower health care costs and fewer missed work and school days.[66] At High Point, a 129-acre (52 ha) mixed-income redevelopment project in Seattle, features to reduce the risk and severity of asthma for residents cost just under $6,000 per unit—a 5 percent or less incremental cost—and resulted in a two-thirds decrease in the number of days missed from school or work.[67]

Another low-cost, but effective, healthy investment is simply installing signage that encourages stair use, which can increase physical activity.[68] Energy- and water-saving features—such as placing windows in locations that optimize natural light and providing natural ventilation that prevents overheating or excessive cooling—can reduce utility bills, which are disproportionately burdensome for low-income families.[69]

Regardless of project type, stage of development, and budget, a wide range of health-promoting features and programs are possible. Residents reap the health benefits—and building owners realize the associated cost savings and marketing advantages.

HEALTHY HOUSING SUPPORTS RESIDENT STABILITY AND WELL-BEING

Health-promoting housing features incorporated within affordable and mixed-income projects result in satisfied residents who are more likely to want to, and be able to, remain. Such improved resident stability—which is valuable for developers and owners of rental properties across the housing marketplace—sustains the overall bottom line.

For example, investing in indoor and outdoor communal gathering areas can establish a sense of community and reduce social isolation, while also driving resident retention and minimizing turnover.[70] Turnover is a leading contributor to operating expenses for several reasons: unit preparation costs, marketing costs, and other expenses.[71]

Evidence also confirms that resident instability disrupts social ties.[72] The existence of strong social connections in one's life has been shown to be as essential as getting an adequate amount of sleep, eating nutritiously, and not smoking. The evidence shows that people who have satisfying relationships are happier, have fewer health issues, and live longer.[73]

> **"** We are now including health and community-farming initiatives at many of our properties because it's the right thing to do, and we are getting a very strong positive response. Residents are telling us that they are staying at our properties and renewing leases specifically because of the health-promoting amenities and programs we have in place. **"**

Blake Olafson
Founder and Managing Partner, ACRE (Asia Capital Real Estate)

Palms at Cedar Trace | Tampa, Florida
Asia Capital Real Estate

Greenbridge | King County, Washington
King County Housing Authority

POTENTIAL BENEFITS FOR DEVELOPERS FROM INVESTING IN HEALTH IN THEIR PROJECTS

Planning and design	Project marketing	Project completion	Operations and maintenance
• Stronger support for proposed developments through early community engagement related to healthy features and programs	• Ability to capture strong market demand for health	• Potential for accelerated market absorption rates	• Potential increased net operating income
• Increased buy-in from all stakeholders, including residents, public officials, and investors	• Increased marketability from project differentiation	• Potential for enhanced asset value through faster lease-ups and sales	• Relatively low operational expenditures for healthy features compared with some project amenities
• Faster zoning approvals and entitlements in certain jurisdictions, thereby lowering project costs	• Ability to create project branding based on health and well-being	• Ability to optimize sales or rental rates	• Long-term cost savings through energy- and water-saving features
• Increased ability to attract social impact investment	• Increased project visibility due to media attention	• Relatively low capital expenditures on healthy features compared with some other "traditional" amenities	• Potential for increased residential tenant retention
	• Ability to enhance project branding or burnish a firm's reputation through high-quality design		• Sustained long-term real estate value

NOTES

1. Urban Land Institute, *America in 2015: A ULI Survey of Views on Housing, Transportation, and Community* (Washington, DC: Urban Land Institute, 2015).

2. American Planning Association, "Investing in Place for Economic Growth and Competitiveness," May 2014, https://planning-org-uploaded-media. s3.amazonaws.com/legacy_resources/policy/polls/ investing/pdf/pollinvestingreport.pdf.

3. David Bassett et al., "Architectural Design and Physical Activity: An Observational Study of Staircase and Elevator Use in Different Buildings," *Journal of Physical Activity and Health* 10, no. 4 (2013): 556–62.

4. Robin E. Soler et al., "Point-of-Decision Prompts to Increase Stair Use: A Systematic Review Update," *American Journal of Preventive Medicine* 38, suppl. *2* (2010): S292–S300, https:// doi.org/10.1016/j.amepre.2009.10.028.

5. National Apartment Association, "Adding Value in the Age of Amenities Wars," 2017, www.naahq. org/sites/default/files/naa-documents/government-affairs/naa_valueaddamenities_2017_final-r.pdf.

6. Transportation Alternatives and Rack & Go, "Bicycle Parking Solutions: A Resource for Improving Secure Bicycle Parking in New York City," https://www.transalt.org/sites/default/files/ issues/bike/bikeparking.pdf.

7. National Apartment Association, "Adding Value in the Age of Amenities Wars," 2017, www.naahq. org/sites/default/files/naa-documents/government-affairs/naa_valueaddamenities_2017_final-r.pdf.

8. Marla Reicks et al., "Impact of Cooking and Home Food Preparation Interventions among Adults: Outcomes and Implications for Future Programs," *Journal of Nutrition Education and Behavior* 46, no. 4 (2014): 259–76.

9. ChangeLab Solutions, "Working with Landlords and Property Managers on Smoke-Free Housing," 2014, www.changelabsolutions.org/sites/default/ files/SFMUH_Guidebook_FINAL_20140417.pdf.

10. Greg D. Ander, "Daylighting," Whole Building Design Guide (website), National Institute of Building Sciences, 2016, www.wbdg.org/ resources/daylighting.

11. YongMin Cho et al., "Effects of Artificial Light at Night on Human Health: A Literature Review of Observational and Experimental Studies Applied to Exposure Assessment," *Chronobiology International* 32, no. 9 (2015): 1294–1310.

12. Anita Kramer et al., *Building for Wellness: The Business Case* (Washington, DC: Urban Land Institute, 2014).

13. U.S. Environmental Protection Agency, *The Inside Story: A Guide to Indoor Air Quality* (Washington, DC: U.S. Environmental Protection Agency, 1995).

14. Tim K. Takaro et al., "The Breathe-Easy Home: The Impact of Asthma-Friendly Home Construction on Clinical Outcomes and Trigger Exposure," *American Journal of Public Health* 101, no. 1 (2011): 55–62.

15. J Turner Research, *Resident Lifestyle Preferences: An Insight* (Houston, TX: J Turner Research, 2014), www.jturnerresearch.com/hubfs/Docs/ ResidentLifestylePreferencesSeptember2014.pdf.

16. National Multifamily Housing Council and Kingsley Associates, "2017 NMHC/Kingsley Apartment Renter Preferences Report," 2017.

17. American Planning Association, "Investing in Place for Economic Growth and Competitiveness," May 2014, https://planning-org-uploaded-media. s3.amazonaws.com/legacy_resources/policy/polls/ investing/pdf/pollinvestingreport.pdf.

18. Michael Andersen, "Salt Lake City Street Removes Parking, Adds Bike Lanes and Sales Go Up," PeopleForBikes, October 5, 2015, https:// peopleforbikes.org/blog/salt-lake-city-street-removes-parking-adds-bike-lanes-and-sales-go-up/.

19. Urban Land Institute, *Implementing Creative Placemaking in Real Estate* (Washington, DC: Urban Land Institute, 2016).

20. Christine Haigh and Jackie Schneider, "Thirsty Play: A Survey of Drinking Water Provision in Public Parks," Children's Food Campaign, 2010.

21. Federal Highway Administration, "Safety Benefits of Walkways, Sidewalks, and Paved Shoulders," 2013, https://safety.fhwa.dot.gov/ped_bike/tools_ solve/walkways_brochure/walkways_brochure.pdf.

22. Thomas Gotschi, "Costs and Benefits of Bicycling Investments in Portland, Oregon," *Journal of Physical Activity and Health* 8, suppl. 1 (2011): S49–S58.

23. Urban Land Institute, *Building Healthy Places Toolkit: Strategies for Enhancing Health in the Built Environment* (Washington, DC: Urban Land Institute, 2015).

24. McGraw Hill Construction, *The Drive toward Healthier Buildings: The Market Drivers and Impact of Building Design and Construction on Occupant Health, Well-Being and Productivity* (Bedford, MA: McGraw Hill Construction, 2014); Urban Land Institute, *America in 2013: A ULI Survey of Views on Housing, Transportation, and Community* (Washington, DC: Urban Land Institute, 2013).

25. Aaron Chalfin et al., "The Impact of Street Lighting on Crime in New York City Public Housing," University of Chicago Crime Lab New York, 2017, https://dokumen.tips/documents/the-impact-of-street-lighting-on-crime-the-impact-of-street-lighting-on-crime.html.

26. National Gardening Association, "Garden to Table: A 5-Year Look at Food Gardening in America," 2014, https://garden.org/special/ pdf/2014-NGA-Garden-to-Table.pdf.

27. Nancy Henkin, Corita Brown, and Sally Leiderman, "Communities for All Ages: Intergenerational Community Building—Lessons Learned," Intergenerational Center, Temple University, June 2012, https://www.aarp.org/content/dam/aarp/ livable-communities/learn/civic/intergenerational-community-building-lessons-learned-aarp.pdf.

28. April Philips, *Designing Urban Agriculture: A Complete Guide to the Planning, Design, Construction, Maintenance, and Management of Edible Landscapes* (Hoboken, NJ: John Wiley, 2013).

29. Tim Blackwell, "The Hottest Trends in Multifamily Outdoor Living," *Property Management Insider*, March 26, 2016, https://www. propertymanagementinsider.com/the-hottest-trends-in-multifamily-outdoor-living.

30. Robert Breunig, Syed Hasan, and Kym Whiteoak, "Impact of Playgrounds on Property Prices: Evidence from Australia," March 4, 2018, https://crawford.anu.edu.au/files/uploads/crawford01_cap_anu_edu_au/2018-04/playgrounds_wp_march2018.pdf.

31. American Society of Landscape Architects, "ASLA Survey: Demand High for Residential Landscapes with Sustainability and Active Living Elements," April 3, 2018, https://www.asla.org/NewsReleaseDetails.aspx?id=53135.

32. Janet Clements et al., "The Green Edge: How Commercial Property Investment in Green Infrastructure Creates Value," National Resources Defense Council, December 2013, https://www.nrdc.org/sites/default/files/commercial-value-green-infrastructure-report.pdf.

33. Judith Bell et al., *Access to Healthy Food and Why It Matters: A Review of the Research* (Oakland, CA: PolicyLink and The Food Trust, 2013), http://thefoodtrust.org/uploads/media_items/access-to-healthy-food.original.pdf.

34. Urban Land Institute, *America in 2015: A ULI Survey of Views on Housing, Transportation, and Community* (Washington, DC: Urban Land Institute, 2015).

35. Todd Litman, "Low Crime Rates in Large Cities Support Multi-Modal Planning and Smart Growth," *Planetizen Interchange* (blog), October 31, 2013, https://www.planetizen.com/node/65857.

36. Urban Land Institute, *America in 2015: A ULI Survey of Views on Housing, Transportation, and Community* (Washington, DC: Urban Land Institute, 2015).

37. Greg D. Ander, "Daylighting," Whole Building Design Guide (website), National Institute of Building Sciences, 2016, www.wbdg.org/resources/daylighting.

38. Anita Kramer et al., *Building for Wellness: The Business Case* (Washington, DC: Urban Land Institute, 2014).

39. "Building Healthy Places," *PD&R Edge*, 2017, https://www.huduser.gov/portal/pdredge/pdr-edge-featd-article-102317.html.

40. Natalie Orenstein, "A Ride to Better Health," *Crosswalk Magazine*, May 25, 2017, https://medium.com/bhpn-crosswalk/a-ride-to-better-health-7a41dd8d338e; Denver Housing Authority, "The Healthy Development Measurement Tool (HDMT) at South Lincoln Homes Redevelopment," 2018, www.denverhousing.org/development/Mariposa/Documents/HDMT%20Summary%20Brochure.pdf.

41. Centers for Disease Control and Prevention, Health Impact Assessment, September 19, 2016, www.cdc.gov/healthyplaces/hia.htm.

42. "White Center's Sustainable Urban Village," GGLO Design, 2018, www.gglo.com/places/greenbridge/.

43. Denver Housing Authority and Mithun Inc., "Mariposa Healthy Living Toolkit," 2012, www.denverhousing.org/development/Mariposa/Documents/Mariposa%20HLI%20Toolkit%202012.pdf.

44. Erin Douglas, "Denver's Mariposa District Leads Charge in Changing the Face of Public Housing," *Denver Post,* August 4, 2017, https://www.denverpost.com/2017/08/04/mariposa-district-denver-public-housing/.

45. Erin Douglas, "Denver's Mariposa District Leads Charge in Changing the Face of Public Housing," *Denver Post,* August 4, 2017, https://www.denverpost.com/2017/08/04/mariposa-district-denver-public-housing/.

46. Urban Land Institute, "Mariposa: Denver, Colorado," 2015, http://bhptoolkit.uli.org/wp-content/uploads/2015/04/Mariposa.pdf.

47. Steven Cummins, Ellen Flint, and Stephen A. Matthews, "New Neighborhood Grocery Store Increased Awareness of Food Access but Did Not Alter Dietary Habits or Obesity," Health Affairs 33, no. 2 (2014): 283–91, doi: 10.1377/hlthaff.2013.0512.

48. National Apartment Association, "Adding Value in the Age of Amenities Wars," 2017, www.naahq.org/sites/default/files/naa-documents/government-affairs/naa_valueaddamenities_2017_final-r.pdf.

49. Urban Land Institute, "New Genesis Apartments: Los Angeles, California," 2017, https://americas.uli.org/wp-content/uploads/sites/125/ULI-Documents/New-Genesis-Apartments.pdf.

50. "Inside Atlanta: Eastlake," Purpose Built Communities," https://purposebuiltcommunities.org/our-network/atlanta-east-lake/.

51. Pamela Miller, "Atlanta Supports Villages of East Lake Affordable Housing," August 31, 2018, https://www.ajc.com/news/local/atlanta-supports-villages-east-lake-affordable-housing/H5a5QLVl5HJGfRg6nDzPol/.

52. Jeni Miller, "The Villages of East Lake, Atlanta, Georgia," *Build Healthy Places* (blog), October 11, 2017, https://buildhealthyplaces.org/whats-new/the-villages-of-east-lake-atlanta-georgia/.

53. Chrissa Pagitsas, "How Much Greener Can Multifamily Get in 2018," Fannie Mae website, February 7, 2018, https://www.fanniemae.com/content/news/mf-green-wire-02072018.

54. Alternatively, borrowers can participate in Healthy Housing Rewards' Enhanced Resident Services pathway, which offers a discount of up to 30 basis points on interest rates—and reimbursement of certification fees—for borrowers who offer resident services to improve the health and stability of residents.

55. Anita Kramer et al., *Building for Wellness: The Business Case* (Washington, DC: Urban Land Institute, 2014).

56. Eric Fisher and Patrick Duke, "Emerging Trends in Healthcare Development: Neighborhood Care, Mixed-Use Models on the Rise," Building Design + Construction, June 5, 3014; Rina Raphael, "Utopic Wellness Communities Are a Multibillion-Dollar Real Estate Trend," Fast Company, January 24, 2018, www.fastcompany.com/40512467/utopic-wellness-communities-are-a-multibillion-dollar-real-estate-trend.

57. National Apartment Association, "Adding Value in the Age of Amenities Wars,"2017, www.naahq.org/sites/default/files/naa-documents/government-affairs/naa_valueaddamenities_2017_final-r.pdf.

58. National Recreation and Park Association, "Americans' Engagement with Parks Survey," 2018, https://www.nrpa.org/publications-research/research-papers/Engagement/.

59. Erin Stepp, "AAA Reveals True Cost of Vehicle Ownership," *AAA NewsRoom*, August 23, 2017, https://newsroom.aaa.com/tag/cost-to-own-a-vehicle/.

60. Urban Land Institute, *America in 2015: A ULI Survey of Views on Housing, Transportation, and Community* (Washington, DC: Urban Land Institute, 2015); American Planning Association, "Investing in Place for Economic Growth and Competitiveness," May 2014, https://planning-org-uploaded-media.s3.amazonaws.com/legacy_resources/policy/polls/investing/pdf/pollinvestingreport.pdf; Jerry Ascierto, "Market Movers: How the Emergence of Generation Y, the Aging of Baby Boomers, and Immigration Trends Will Impact the Multifamily Industry in the Next Decade," November 1, 2010, www.multifamilyexecutive.com/property-management/demographics/market-movers_o.

61. Candace Jackson, "Developers Build Luxury, Bike-Friendly Buildings," *Wall Street Journal,* September 25, 2014, https://www.wsj.com/articles/developers-build-luxury-bike-friendly-buildings-1411660659.

62. Amie Winters, "Community Gardens as Amenities," Multifamily Biz, November 1, 2012, https://www.multifamilybiz.com/Blogs/211/Community_Gardens_as_Amenities.

63. Amie Winters, "Community Gardens as Amenities," Multifamily Biz, November 1, 2012, https://www.multifamilybiz.com/Blogs/211/Community_Gardens_as_Amenities; Urban Land Institute, *Cultivating Development: Trends and Opportunities at the Intersection of Food and Real Estate* (Washington, DC: Urban Land Institute, 2016).

64. Urban Land Institute, "Silver Moon Lodge," 2015, https://uli.org/wp-content/uploads/ULI-Documents/Silver-Moon-Lodge.pdf.

65. Urban Land Institute, "Silver Moon Lodge,"2015, https://uli.org/wp-content/uploads/ULI-Documents/Silver-Moon-Lodge.pdf.

66. Tim K. Takaro et al., "The Breathe-Easy Home: The Impact of Asthma-Friendly Home Construction on Clinical Outcomes and Trigger Exposure," *American Journal of Public Health* 101, no. 1 (2011): 55–62.

67. Urban Land Institute, "High Point," 2017, http://bhptoolkit.uli.org/wp-content/uploads/2017/03/High-Point.pdf.

68. Robin E. Soler et al., "Point-of-Decision Prompts to Increase Stair Use: A Systematic Review Update," *American Journal of Preventive Medicine* 38, suppl. 2 (2010): S292–S300, https://doi.org/10.1016/j.amepre.2009.10.028.

69. Catalina Demidchuk, Eric Mackres, and Henrique Evers, "Can Housing Be Affordable without Being Efficient?" World Resources Institute, September 6, 2018, https://www.wri.org/blog/2018/09/can-housing-be-affordable-without-being-efficient.

70. Scott Wickman, "How Multifamily Owners Can Maximize Revenue before Peak Leasing Season," *National Real Estate Investor,* May 30, 2017, https://www.nreionline.com/multifamily/how-multifamily-owners-can-maximize-revenue-peak-leasing-season.

71. Paul Votto, "A 50% Turnover Rate? It's Not High—It's the Average!" National Center for Housing, May 14, 2015, www.nchm.org/Resources/Compliance-Corner/Review/ArticleId/117/A-50-turnover-rate-Its-not-high-its-the-average.

72. Kristin Turney and Kristen Harknett," "Neighborhood Disadvantage, Residential Stability, and Perceptions of Instrumental Support among New Mothers," *Journal of Family Issues* 31, no. 4 (2010): 499–524, doi: 10.1177/0192513X09347992.

73. Harvard Women's Health Watch, "The Health Benefits of Strong Relationships," December 2010, https://www.health.harvard.edu/newsletter_article/the-health-benefits-of-strong-relationships.

Prospect Plaza | Brooklyn, New York
Blue Sea Development and partners

Pavilion Apartments | East Orange, Ne
Vitus Group

Mariposa | Denver, Colorado
Denver Housing Authority

New Genesis Apartments | Los Angele
Skid Row Housing Trust

sey

Greenbridge | King County, Washington
King County Housing Authority

fornia

Villages of East Lake | Atlanta, Georgia
Housing Authority of the City of Atlanta and the East Lake Foundation

ACKNOWLEDGMENTS

We gratefully acknowledge the contributions of ULI members who attended the "Healthy Housing for All" workshop at ULI's 2018 Spring Meeting in Detroit and the following individuals:

Brooke Akins, chief operations officer, Ross Management Group

Mike Alvidrez, chief executive officer, Skid Row Housing Trust

Les Bluestone, president, Blue Sea Development Company and Blue Sea Construction Co.

Eytan Davidson, vice president of communications, Purpose Built Communities

Aruna Doddapaneni, senior vice president, BRIDGE Housing

Jeff Foster, principal, GGLO Design

Ismael Guerrero, executive director, Denver Housing Authority

Erin Christensen Ishizaki, partner, Mithun Inc.

Leah Logan, marketing strategies and communications, multifamily, Fannie Mae

Jessie Lucero, property manager, Silver Moon Lodge

Carol Naughton, president, Purpose Built Communities

George Nemeth, senior housing developer, Seattle Housing Authority

Blake Olafson, founder and managing partner, ACRE (Asia Capital Real Estate)

John Pettigrew, regional manager, Ross Management Group

Sharon Roerty, senior program officer, Robert Wood Johnson Foundation

Sue Setliff, special projects, ACRE (Asia Capital Real Estate)

Anne M. Torney, partner, Mithun Inc.

Dana Trujillo, chief investment and finance officer, Skid Row Housing Trust

Kathryn "Katie" Wehr, senior program officer, Robert Wood Johnson Foundation

Stephen Whyte, founder and managing director, Vitus Group